50 Pancake and Waffle Recipes

By: Kelly Johnson

Table of Contents

- Classic Buttermilk Pancakes
- Fluffy Chocolate Chip Pancakes
- Blueberry Pancakes
- Banana Nut Pancakes
- Whole Wheat Pancakes
- Red Velvet Pancakes
- Cinnamon Roll Pancakes
- Lemon Poppy Seed Pancakes
- Apple Cinnamon Pancakes
- Pumpkin Spice Pancakes
- Protein-Packed Pancakes
- Sweet Potato Pancakes
- Carrot Cake Pancakes
- Strawberry Shortcake Pancakes
- Almond Joy Pancakes
- Maple Bacon Pancakes
- Peanut Butter Banana Pancakes
- Mocha Pancakes
- Nutella Stuffed Pancakes
- Churro Pancakes
- Ricotta Pancakes
- Coconut Pancakes
- Cherry Almond Pancakes
- S'mores Pancakes
- Matcha Pancakes
- Lemon Blueberry Waffles
- Classic Belgian Waffles
- Chocolate Waffles
- Banana Waffles
- Strawberry Waffles
- Red Velvet Waffles
- Savory Herb Waffles
- Pumpkin Waffles
- Cinnamon Roll Waffles
- Almond Waffles

- Coconut Waffles
- Apple Pie Waffles
- S'mores Waffles
- Buttermilk Waffles
- Pecan Waffles
- Bacon Cheddar Waffles
- Gingerbread Waffles
- Mocha Waffles
- Raspberry Chocolate Waffles
- Protein-Packed Waffles
- Banana Nut Waffles
- Spiced Pear Waffles
- Lemon Ricotta Waffles
- Vanilla Bean Waffles
- Blueberry Cheesecake Waffles

Classic Buttermilk Pancakes

Ingredients:

- 1 cup all-purpose flour
- 1 tbsp sugar
- 1 tsp baking powder
- ½ tsp baking soda
- ½ tsp salt
- 1 cup buttermilk
- 1 egg
- 2 tbsp melted butter

Instructions:

1. In a bowl, mix flour, sugar, baking powder, baking soda, and salt.
2. In a separate bowl, whisk buttermilk, egg, and melted butter.
3. Pour the wet ingredients into the dry ingredients and stir until just combined.
4. Heat a non-stick skillet over medium heat and lightly grease it.
5. Pour ¼ cup of batter onto the skillet for each pancake.
6. Cook until bubbles form on the surface, then flip and cook for another 1-2 minutes.
7. Serve warm with syrup.

Fluffy Chocolate Chip Pancakes

Ingredients:

- 1 cup all-purpose flour
- 1 tbsp sugar
- 1 tsp baking powder
- 1/2 tsp baking soda
- ½ tsp salt
- 1 cup buttermilk
- 1 egg
- 1 tsp vanilla extract
- ½ cup mini chocolate chips

Instructions:

1. Mix flour, sugar, baking powder, baking soda, and salt in a bowl.
2. In another bowl, whisk together buttermilk, egg, and vanilla.
3. Stir the wet ingredients into the dry ingredients until just combined.
4. Gently fold in chocolate chips.
5. Cook on a greased skillet over medium heat, using ¼ cup of batter per pancake.
6. Flip when bubbles appear and cook for another 1-2 minutes.
7. Serve with chocolate syrup or whipped cream.

Blueberry Pancakes

Ingredients:

- 1 cup all-purpose flour
- 1 tbsp sugar
- 1 tsp baking powder
- ½ tsp baking soda
- ½ tsp salt
- 1 cup buttermilk
- 1 egg
- 2 tbsp melted butter
- ½ cup fresh blueberries

Instructions:

1. Mix flour, sugar, baking powder, baking soda, and salt in a bowl.
2. In another bowl, whisk together buttermilk, egg, and melted butter.
3. Combine the wet and dry ingredients, then gently fold in blueberries.
4. Heat a non-stick skillet over medium heat and lightly grease it.
5. Pour ¼ cup of batter for each pancake and cook until bubbles appear, then flip.
6. Cook until golden brown and serve with maple syrup.

Banana Nut Pancakes

Ingredients:

- 1 cup all-purpose flour
- 1 tbsp sugar
- 1 tsp baking powder
- ½ tsp baking soda
- ½ tsp salt
- 1 cup buttermilk
- 1 egg
- 1 ripe banana, mashed
- ¼ cup chopped walnuts

Instructions:

1. Mix flour, sugar, baking powder, baking soda, and salt in a bowl.
2. In another bowl, whisk buttermilk, egg, and mashed banana.
3. Add the wet ingredients to the dry ingredients and stir to combine.
4. Fold in chopped walnuts.
5. Cook pancakes on a greased skillet over medium heat until golden brown, flipping once.
6. Serve with extra banana slices and syrup.

Whole Wheat Pancakes

Ingredients:

- 1 cup whole wheat flour
- 1 tbsp sugar
- 1 tsp baking powder
- ½ tsp baking soda
- ½ tsp salt
- 1 cup buttermilk
- 1 egg
- 2 tbsp melted butter

Instructions:

1. In a bowl, combine whole wheat flour, sugar, baking powder, baking soda, and salt.
2. In a separate bowl, whisk together buttermilk, egg, and melted butter.
3. Stir the wet ingredients into the dry ingredients until just combined.
4. Heat a non-stick skillet over medium heat and lightly grease it.
5. Pour ¼ cup of batter per pancake and cook until bubbles form, then flip.
6. Serve with fresh fruit and syrup.

Red Velvet Pancakes

Ingredients:

- 1 cup all-purpose flour
- 2 tbsp sugar
- 1 tsp baking powder
- ½ tsp baking soda
- 1 tbsp cocoa powder
- 1 egg
- 1 cup buttermilk
- 2 tbsp red food coloring
- 2 tbsp melted butter

Instructions:

1. In a bowl, mix flour, sugar, baking powder, baking soda, and cocoa powder.
2. In another bowl, whisk buttermilk, egg, red food coloring, and melted butter.
3. Combine the wet and dry ingredients and mix until smooth.
4. Cook pancakes on a greased skillet over medium heat, flipping when bubbles appear.
5. Serve with cream cheese frosting or whipped cream.

Cinnamon Roll Pancakes

Ingredients:

- 1 cup all-purpose flour
- 1 tbsp sugar
- 1 tsp baking powder
- ½ tsp baking soda
- ½ tsp cinnamon
- 1 cup buttermilk
- 1 egg
- 2 tbsp melted butter
- ½ cup cinnamon swirl (mix cinnamon, sugar, and melted butter)
- Glaze: ¼ cup powdered sugar, 1 tbsp milk, ½ tsp vanilla

Instructions:

1. Mix flour, sugar, baking powder, baking soda, and cinnamon in a bowl.
2. In another bowl, whisk buttermilk, egg, and melted butter.
3. Stir the wet ingredients into the dry ingredients until smooth.
4. Heat a non-stick skillet over medium heat and lightly grease it.
5. Pour pancake batter onto the skillet and swirl the cinnamon mixture on top.
6. Flip when bubbles appear and cook until golden.
7. Drizzle with glaze and serve.

Lemon Poppy Seed Pancakes

Ingredients:

- 1 cup all-purpose flour
- 1 tbsp sugar
- 1 tsp baking powder
- ½ tsp baking soda
- 1 tsp lemon zest
- 1 tbsp poppy seeds
- 1 cup buttermilk
- 1 egg
- 2 tbsp melted butter

Instructions:

1. Mix flour, sugar, baking powder, baking soda, lemon zest, and poppy seeds in a bowl.
2. In another bowl, whisk together buttermilk, egg, and melted butter.
3. Stir the wet ingredients into the dry ingredients until combined.
4. Cook pancakes on a greased skillet over medium heat until golden, flipping once.
5. Serve with fresh lemon slices and syrup.

Apple Cinnamon Pancakes

Ingredients:

- 1 cup all-purpose flour
- 1 tbsp sugar
- 1 tsp baking powder
- ½ tsp baking soda
- ½ tsp cinnamon
- 1 cup buttermilk
- 1 egg
- 1 apple, grated
- 2 tbsp melted butter

Instructions:

1. Mix flour, sugar, baking powder, baking soda, and cinnamon in a bowl.
2. In a separate bowl, whisk buttermilk, egg, and melted butter.
3. Stir the wet ingredients into the dry ingredients, then fold in the grated apple.
4. Cook pancakes on a greased skillet over medium heat, flipping once.
5. Serve with cinnamon sugar or maple syrup.

Pumpkin Spice Pancakes

Ingredients:

- 1 cup all-purpose flour
- 1 tbsp sugar
- 1 tsp baking powder
- ½ tsp baking soda
- 1 tsp pumpkin pie spice
- 1 cup buttermilk
- 1 egg
- ½ cup pumpkin puree
- 2 tbsp melted butter

Instructions:

1. Mix flour, sugar, baking powder, baking soda, and pumpkin pie spice in a bowl.
2. In another bowl, whisk buttermilk, egg, pumpkin puree, and melted butter.
3. Combine the wet and dry ingredients until smooth.
4. Cook pancakes on a greased skillet over medium heat, flipping once.
5. Serve with whipped cream or maple syrup.

Protein-Packed Pancakes

Ingredients:

- 1 cup oats
- ½ cup cottage cheese
- 2 eggs
- 1 tsp vanilla extract
- 1 tbsp honey
- 1 tsp baking powder

Instructions:

1. Blend oats in a food processor until fine.
2. Mix with cottage cheese, eggs, vanilla, honey, and baking powder until smooth.
3. Cook pancakes on a greased skillet over medium heat until golden.
4. Serve with fresh fruit and syrup for added flavor.

Sweet Potato Pancakes

Ingredients:

- 1 cup all-purpose flour
- 1 tsp baking powder
- ½ tsp baking soda
- 1 tsp cinnamon
- ¼ tsp nutmeg
- 1 cup mashed sweet potato
- 1 egg
- 1 cup buttermilk
- 2 tbsp melted butter

Instructions:

1. In a bowl, mix flour, baking powder, baking soda, cinnamon, and nutmeg.
2. In another bowl, whisk together mashed sweet potato, egg, buttermilk, and melted butter.
3. Combine wet and dry ingredients until smooth.
4. Cook pancakes on a greased skillet over medium heat, flipping once.
5. Serve with maple syrup or whipped cream.

Carrot Cake Pancakes

Ingredients:

- 1 cup all-purpose flour
- 1 tsp baking powder
- 1 tsp cinnamon
- ¼ tsp nutmeg
- 1 egg
- 1 cup grated carrots
- ½ cup buttermilk
- 1 tsp vanilla extract
- ¼ cup walnuts, chopped
- Cream cheese glaze (optional)

Instructions:

1. In a bowl, mix flour, baking powder, cinnamon, and nutmeg.
2. In another bowl, whisk together egg, grated carrots, buttermilk, and vanilla.
3. Stir the wet ingredients into the dry ingredients.
4. Fold in chopped walnuts.
5. Cook pancakes on a greased skillet over medium heat, flipping once.
6. Drizzle with cream cheese glaze and serve immediately.

Strawberry Shortcake Pancakes

Ingredients:

- 1 cup all-purpose flour
- 1 tbsp sugar
- 1 tsp baking powder
- 1 egg
- 1 cup buttermilk
- ½ tsp vanilla extract
- Fresh strawberries, sliced
- Whipped cream

Instructions:

1. In a bowl, mix flour, sugar, and baking powder.
2. In another bowl, whisk together egg, buttermilk, and vanilla.
3. Combine the wet and dry ingredients until smooth.
4. Cook pancakes on a greased skillet over medium heat, flipping once.
5. Top with sliced strawberries and whipped cream.

Almond Joy Pancakes

Ingredients:

- 1 cup all-purpose flour
- 1 tsp baking powder
- 1 tbsp cocoa powder
- ¼ cup shredded coconut
- ¼ cup chopped almonds
- 1 egg
- 1 cup milk
- 1 tsp vanilla extract
- Chocolate syrup or Nutella for drizzling

Instructions:

1. In a bowl, mix flour, baking powder, cocoa powder, coconut, and almonds.
2. In another bowl, whisk together egg, milk, and vanilla.
3. Combine the wet and dry ingredients until smooth.
4. Cook pancakes on a greased skillet over medium heat, flipping once.
5. Drizzle with chocolate syrup or Nutella.

Maple Bacon Pancakes

Ingredients:

- 1 cup all-purpose flour
- 1 tsp baking powder
- ½ tsp baking soda
- 1 egg
- 1 cup buttermilk
- 2 tbsp melted butter
- ½ cup cooked bacon, crumbled
- Maple syrup for serving

Instructions:

1. In a bowl, mix flour, baking powder, and baking soda.
2. In another bowl, whisk together egg, buttermilk, and melted butter.
3. Stir the wet ingredients into the dry ingredients.
4. Fold in crumbled bacon.
5. Cook pancakes on a greased skillet over medium heat, flipping once.
6. Serve with maple syrup.

Peanut Butter Banana Pancakes

Ingredients:

- 1 cup all-purpose flour
- 1 tbsp sugar
- 1 tsp baking powder
- 1 egg
- 1 cup milk
- 2 tbsp peanut butter
- 1 banana, sliced

Instructions:

1. In a bowl, mix flour, sugar, and baking powder.
2. In another bowl, whisk together egg, milk, and peanut butter.
3. Combine wet and dry ingredients until smooth.
4. Cook pancakes on a greased skillet over medium heat, flipping once.
5. Top with banana slices and serve.

Mocha Pancakes

Ingredients:

- 1 cup all-purpose flour
- 1 tbsp sugar
- 1 tsp baking powder
- 1 tsp cocoa powder
- 1 tbsp instant coffee granules
- 1 egg
- 1 cup milk
- 1 tsp vanilla extract

Instructions:

1. In a bowl, mix flour, sugar, baking powder, cocoa powder, and coffee granules.
2. In another bowl, whisk together egg, milk, and vanilla.
3. Stir the wet ingredients into the dry ingredients until smooth.
4. Cook pancakes on a greased skillet over medium heat, flipping once.
5. Serve with whipped cream or chocolate syrup.

Nutella Stuffed Pancakes

Ingredients:

- 1 cup all-purpose flour
- 1 tbsp sugar
- 1 tsp baking powder
- 1 egg
- 1 cup milk
- Nutella for stuffing

Instructions:

1. In a bowl, mix flour, sugar, and baking powder.
2. In another bowl, whisk together egg and milk.
3. Stir the wet ingredients into the dry ingredients until smooth.
4. Pour pancake batter onto the skillet, add a spoonful of Nutella in the center, and cover with more batter.
5. Cook on both sides until golden brown.
6. Serve with extra Nutella.

Churro Pancakes

Ingredients:

- 1 cup all-purpose flour
- 1 tbsp sugar
- 1 tsp baking powder
- ½ tsp cinnamon
- 1 egg
- 1 cup milk
- 2 tbsp melted butter
- Cinnamon sugar for topping

Instructions:

1. In a bowl, mix flour, sugar, baking powder, and cinnamon.
2. In another bowl, whisk together egg, milk, and melted butter.
3. Combine the wet and dry ingredients until smooth.
4. Cook pancakes on a greased skillet over medium heat, flipping once.
5. Sprinkle with cinnamon sugar and serve.

Ricotta Pancakes

Ingredients:

- 1 cup all-purpose flour
- 1 tsp baking powder
- 1 egg
- 1 cup ricotta cheese
- 1 cup milk
- 1 tsp vanilla extract
- 1 tbsp sugar

Instructions:

1. In a bowl, mix flour and baking powder.
2. In another bowl, whisk together egg, ricotta cheese, milk, vanilla, and sugar.
3. Combine the wet and dry ingredients until smooth.
4. Cook pancakes on a greased skillet over medium heat, flipping once.
5. Serve with syrup or fresh fruit.

Coconut Pancakes

Ingredients:

- 1 cup all-purpose flour
- 1 tbsp sugar
- 1 tsp baking powder
- ½ tsp baking soda
- ¼ tsp salt
- 1 cup coconut milk
- 1 egg
- ½ cup shredded coconut

Instructions:

1. In a bowl, mix flour, sugar, baking powder, baking soda, and salt.
2. In another bowl, whisk together coconut milk and egg.
3. Stir the wet ingredients into the dry ingredients until just combined.
4. Gently fold in shredded coconut.
5. Cook pancakes on a greased skillet over medium heat, flipping once.
6. Serve with extra coconut or syrup.

Cherry Almond Pancakes

Ingredients:

- 1 cup all-purpose flour
- 1 tbsp sugar
- 1 tsp baking powder
- ½ tsp baking soda
- ½ tsp almond extract
- 1 cup buttermilk
- 1 egg
- ½ cup fresh or dried cherries, chopped
- 2 tbsp sliced almonds

Instructions:

1. In a bowl, mix flour, sugar, baking powder, and baking soda.
2. In another bowl, whisk together almond extract, buttermilk, and egg.
3. Combine wet and dry ingredients until smooth.
4. Gently fold in cherries and sliced almonds.
5. Cook pancakes on a greased skillet over medium heat, flipping once.
6. Serve with additional cherries or almonds on top.

S'mores Pancakes

Ingredients:

- 1 cup all-purpose flour
- 1 tbsp sugar
- 1 tsp baking powder
- 1/2 tsp baking soda
- ¼ cup mini marshmallows
- ¼ cup chocolate chips
- 2 tbsp graham cracker crumbs
- 1 cup buttermilk
- 1 egg

Instructions:

1. In a bowl, mix flour, sugar, baking powder, and baking soda.
2. In another bowl, whisk together buttermilk and egg.
3. Stir the wet ingredients into the dry ingredients until just combined.
4. Fold in marshmallows, chocolate chips, and graham cracker crumbs.
5. Cook pancakes on a greased skillet over medium heat, flipping once.
6. Serve with more marshmallows and chocolate drizzle on top.

Matcha Pancakes

Ingredients:

- 1 cup all-purpose flour
- 1 tbsp sugar
- 1 tsp baking powder
- 1 tsp matcha powder
- 1 cup milk
- 1 egg
- 1 tsp vanilla extract

Instructions:

1. In a bowl, mix flour, sugar, baking powder, and matcha powder.
2. In another bowl, whisk together milk, egg, and vanilla.
3. Stir the wet ingredients into the dry ingredients until smooth.
4. Cook pancakes on a greased skillet over medium heat, flipping once.
5. Serve with whipped cream or a drizzle of honey.

Lemon Blueberry Waffles

Ingredients:

- 1 ½ cups all-purpose flour
- 1 tbsp sugar
- 1 tsp baking powder
- ½ tsp baking soda
- ½ tsp salt
- 1 cup buttermilk
- 2 eggs
- 2 tbsp melted butter
- 1 tsp lemon zest
- ½ cup fresh blueberries

Instructions:

1. Preheat your waffle iron.
2. In a bowl, mix flour, sugar, baking powder, baking soda, and salt.
3. In another bowl, whisk together buttermilk, eggs, melted butter, and lemon zest.
4. Stir the wet ingredients into the dry ingredients, then fold in blueberries.
5. Pour batter into the waffle iron and cook according to the manufacturer's instructions.
6. Serve with fresh blueberries and syrup.

Classic Belgian Waffles

Ingredients:

- 2 cups all-purpose flour
- 2 tbsp sugar
- 1 tbsp baking powder
- ¼ tsp salt
- 1 ½ cups milk
- 2 eggs
- ½ cup melted butter
- 1 tsp vanilla extract

Instructions:

1. Preheat your waffle iron.
2. In a bowl, mix flour, sugar, baking powder, and salt.
3. In another bowl, whisk together milk, eggs, melted butter, and vanilla.
4. Stir the wet ingredients into the dry ingredients until smooth.
5. Pour batter into the waffle iron and cook according to the manufacturer's instructions.
6. Serve with syrup, whipped cream, or berries.

Chocolate Waffles

Ingredients:

- 1 ½ cups all-purpose flour
- 2 tbsp cocoa powder
- 2 tbsp sugar
- 1 tsp baking powder
- ½ tsp baking soda
- 1 cup milk
- 2 eggs
- ¼ cup melted chocolate
- 2 tbsp melted butter

Instructions:

1. Preheat your waffle iron.
2. In a bowl, mix flour, cocoa powder, sugar, baking powder, and baking soda.
3. In another bowl, whisk together milk, eggs, melted chocolate, and butter.
4. Stir the wet ingredients into the dry ingredients until smooth.
5. Pour batter into the waffle iron and cook according to the manufacturer's instructions.
6. Serve with chocolate syrup or whipped cream.

Banana Waffles

Ingredients:

- 1 ½ cups all-purpose flour
- 2 tbsp sugar
- 1 tsp baking powder
- 1 tsp cinnamon
- 1 cup milk
- 2 eggs
- 1 ripe banana, mashed
- 2 tbsp melted butter

Instructions:

1. Preheat your waffle iron.
2. In a bowl, mix flour, sugar, baking powder, and cinnamon.
3. In another bowl, whisk together milk, eggs, mashed banana, and melted butter.
4. Stir the wet ingredients into the dry ingredients until smooth.
5. Pour batter into the waffle iron and cook according to the manufacturer's instructions.
6. Serve with banana slices and syrup.

Strawberry Waffles

Ingredients:

- 1 ½ cups all-purpose flour
- 1 tbsp sugar
- 1 tsp baking powder
- ½ tsp baking soda
- 1 cup milk
- 2 eggs
- 1 tsp vanilla extract
- ½ cup fresh strawberries, chopped

Instructions:

1. Preheat your waffle iron.
2. In a bowl, mix flour, sugar, baking powder, and baking soda.
3. In another bowl, whisk together milk, eggs, and vanilla extract.
4. Stir the wet ingredients into the dry ingredients, then fold in chopped strawberries.
5. Pour batter into the waffle iron and cook according to the manufacturer's instructions.
6. Serve with extra strawberries and whipped cream.

Red Velvet Waffles

Ingredients:

- 1 ½ cups all-purpose flour
- 2 tbsp sugar
- 1 tbsp baking powder
- 1 tbsp cocoa powder
- 1 tsp vanilla extract
- 1 cup buttermilk
- 2 eggs
- 2 tbsp red food coloring
- ¼ cup melted butter

Instructions:

1. Preheat your waffle iron.
2. In a bowl, mix flour, sugar, baking powder, and cocoa powder.
3. In another bowl, whisk together buttermilk, eggs, food coloring, and melted butter.
4. Stir the wet ingredients into the dry ingredients until smooth.
5. Pour batter into the waffle iron and cook according to the manufacturer's instructions.
6. Serve with cream cheese frosting or whipped cream.

Savory Herb Waffles

Ingredients:

- 1 ½ cups all-purpose flour
- 1 tbsp baking powder
- ½ tsp salt
- ½ tsp garlic powder
- 1 tsp dried thyme
- 1 tsp dried rosemary
- 1 cup milk
- 2 eggs
- 2 tbsp melted butter
- ½ cup grated parmesan cheese

Instructions:

1. Preheat your waffle iron.
2. In a bowl, mix flour, baking powder, salt, garlic powder, thyme, rosemary, and parmesan cheese.
3. In another bowl, whisk together milk, eggs, and melted butter.
4. Stir the wet ingredients into the dry ingredients until smooth.
5. Pour batter into the waffle iron and cook according to the manufacturer's instructions.
6. Serve with a dollop of sour cream or your favorite savory topping.

Pumpkin Waffles

Ingredients:

- 1 ½ cups all-purpose flour
- 1 tbsp sugar
- 1 tsp baking powder
- ½ tsp baking soda
- 1 tsp cinnamon
- 1/2 tsp nutmeg
- 1 cup canned pumpkin puree
- 1 cup milk
- 2 eggs
- 2 tbsp melted butter

Instructions:

1. Preheat your waffle iron.
2. In a bowl, mix flour, sugar, baking powder, baking soda, cinnamon, and nutmeg.
3. In another bowl, whisk together pumpkin, milk, eggs, and melted butter.
4. Stir the wet ingredients into the dry ingredients until smooth.
5. Pour batter into the waffle iron and cook according to the manufacturer's instructions.
6. Serve with whipped cream or maple syrup.

Cinnamon Roll Waffles

Ingredients:

- 1 ½ cups all-purpose flour
- 1 tbsp sugar
- 1 tsp baking powder
- 1 tsp cinnamon
- 1 cup milk
- 2 eggs
- 1 tsp vanilla extract
- ¼ cup melted butter
- ¼ cup brown sugar
- 1 tbsp cinnamon (for swirl)

Instructions:

1. Preheat your waffle iron.
2. In a bowl, mix flour, sugar, baking powder, and cinnamon.
3. In another bowl, whisk together milk, eggs, vanilla extract, and melted butter.
4. Stir the wet ingredients into the dry ingredients until smooth.
5. Pour half the batter onto the waffle iron, sprinkle with brown sugar and cinnamon, then add the remaining batter.
6. Cook according to the manufacturer's instructions.
7. Serve with icing or maple syrup.

Almond Waffles

Ingredients:

- 1 ½ cups all-purpose flour
- 1 tbsp sugar
- 1 tsp baking powder
- 1 tsp almond extract
- 1 cup milk
- 2 eggs
- ¼ cup ground almonds
- 2 tbsp melted butter

Instructions:

1. Preheat your waffle iron.
2. In a bowl, mix flour, sugar, baking powder, and ground almonds.
3. In another bowl, whisk together milk, eggs, almond extract, and melted butter.
4. Stir the wet ingredients into the dry ingredients until smooth.
5. Pour batter into the waffle iron and cook according to the manufacturer's instructions.
6. Serve with sliced almonds and honey or maple syrup.

Coconut Waffles

Ingredients:

- 1 ½ cups all-purpose flour
- 1 tbsp sugar
- 1 tsp baking powder
- 1 tsp shredded coconut
- 1 cup coconut milk
- 2 eggs
- 2 tbsp melted butter
- ½ tsp vanilla extract

Instructions:

1. Preheat your waffle iron.
2. In a bowl, mix flour, sugar, baking powder, and shredded coconut.
3. In another bowl, whisk together coconut milk, eggs, melted butter, and vanilla extract.
4. Stir the wet ingredients into the dry ingredients until smooth.
5. Pour batter into the waffle iron and cook according to the manufacturer's instructions.
6. Serve with toasted coconut flakes and syrup.

Apple Pie Waffles

Ingredients:

- 1 ½ cups all-purpose flour
- 1 tbsp sugar
- 1 tsp baking powder
- 1 tsp cinnamon
- ½ tsp nutmeg
- 1 cup milk
- 2 eggs
- 1 apple, diced and sautéed in cinnamon sugar
- 2 tbsp melted butter

Instructions:

1. Preheat your waffle iron.
2. In a bowl, mix flour, sugar, baking powder, cinnamon, and nutmeg.
3. In another bowl, whisk together milk, eggs, and melted butter.
4. Stir the wet ingredients into the dry ingredients until smooth.
5. Fold in sautéed apple pieces.
6. Pour batter into the waffle iron and cook according to the manufacturer's instructions.
7. Serve with whipped cream or vanilla ice cream.

S'mores Waffles

Ingredients:

- 1 ½ cups all-purpose flour
- 1 tbsp sugar
- 1 tsp baking powder
- 2 tbsp cocoa powder
- ½ cup mini marshmallows
- ½ cup chocolate chips
- 1 cup milk
- 2 eggs
- 2 tbsp melted butter

Instructions:

1. Preheat your waffle iron.
2. In a bowl, mix flour, sugar, baking powder, and cocoa powder.
3. In another bowl, whisk together milk, eggs, and melted butter.
4. Stir the wet ingredients into the dry ingredients until smooth.
5. Fold in mini marshmallows and chocolate chips.
6. Pour batter into the waffle iron and cook according to the manufacturer's instructions.
7. Serve with extra marshmallows and chocolate drizzle.

Buttermilk Waffles

Ingredients:

- 2 cups all-purpose flour
- 1 tbsp sugar
- 1 tsp baking powder
- ½ tsp baking soda
- ¼ tsp salt
- 1 ½ cups buttermilk
- 2 eggs
- ¼ cup melted butter

Instructions:

1. Preheat your waffle iron.
2. In a bowl, mix flour, sugar, baking powder, baking soda, and salt.
3. In another bowl, whisk together buttermilk, eggs, and melted butter.
4. Stir the wet ingredients into the dry ingredients until smooth.
5. Pour batter into the waffle iron and cook according to the manufacturer's instructions.
6. Serve with butter and syrup.

Pecan Waffles

Ingredients:

- 1 ½ cups all-purpose flour
- 1 tbsp sugar
- 1 tsp baking powder
- ½ tsp baking soda
- ¼ tsp salt
- 1 cup milk
- 2 eggs
- ½ cup chopped pecans
- 2 tbsp melted butter

Instructions:

1. Preheat your waffle iron.
2. In a bowl, mix flour, sugar, baking powder, baking soda, and salt.
3. In another bowl, whisk together milk, eggs, and melted butter.
4. Stir the wet ingredients into the dry ingredients until smooth.
5. Fold in chopped pecans.
6. Pour batter into the waffle iron and cook according to the manufacturer's instructions.
7. Serve with more chopped pecans and syrup.

Bacon Cheddar Waffles

Ingredients:

- 1 ½ cups all-purpose flour
- 1 tbsp sugar
- 1 tsp baking powder
- ½ tsp baking soda
- ½ tsp salt
- 1 cup milk
- 2 eggs
- 1 cup shredded cheddar cheese
- ½ cup cooked bacon, crumbled
- 2 tbsp melted butter

Instructions:

1. Preheat your waffle iron.
2. In a bowl, mix flour, sugar, baking powder, baking soda, and salt.
3. In another bowl, whisk together milk, eggs, melted butter, and cheddar cheese.
4. Stir the wet ingredients into the dry ingredients until smooth.
5. Fold in crumbled bacon.
6. Pour batter into the waffle iron and cook according to the manufacturer's instructions.
7. Serve with a drizzle of maple syrup.

Gingerbread Waffles

Ingredients:

- 1 ½ cups all-purpose flour
- 1 tbsp sugar
- 1 tsp baking powder
- 1 tsp ground ginger
- 1 tsp cinnamon
- ½ tsp nutmeg
- 1 cup milk
- 2 eggs
- ¼ cup molasses
- 2 tbsp melted butter

Instructions:

1. Preheat your waffle iron.
2. In a bowl, mix flour, sugar, baking powder, ginger, cinnamon, and nutmeg.
3. In another bowl, whisk together milk, eggs, molasses, and melted butter.
4. Stir the wet ingredients into the dry ingredients until smooth.
5. Pour batter into the waffle iron and cook according to the manufacturer's instructions.
6. Serve with whipped cream or molasses drizzle.

Mocha Waffles

Ingredients:

- 1 ½ cups all-purpose flour
- 1 tbsp sugar
- 1 tsp baking powder
- 1 tsp cocoa powder
- 1 tbsp instant coffee granules
- 1 cup milk
- 2 eggs
- 2 tbsp melted butter
- 1 tsp vanilla extract

Instructions:

1. Preheat your waffle iron.
2. In a bowl, mix flour, sugar, baking powder, cocoa powder, and coffee granules.
3. In another bowl, whisk together milk, eggs, melted butter, and vanilla extract.
4. Stir the wet ingredients into the dry ingredients until smooth.
5. Pour batter into the waffle iron and cook according to the manufacturer's instructions.
6. Serve with whipped cream or chocolate syrup.

Raspberry Chocolate Waffles

Ingredients:

- 1 ½ cups all-purpose flour
- 1 tbsp sugar
- 1 tsp baking powder
- 1 tbsp cocoa powder
- ½ cup fresh raspberries
- ½ cup mini chocolate chips
- 1 cup milk
- 2 eggs
- 2 tbsp melted butter

Instructions:

1. Preheat your waffle iron.
2. In a bowl, mix flour, sugar, baking powder, and cocoa powder.
3. In another bowl, whisk together milk, eggs, and melted butter.
4. Stir the wet ingredients into the dry ingredients until smooth.
5. Gently fold in raspberries and chocolate chips.
6. Pour batter into the waffle iron and cook according to the manufacturer's instructions.
7. Serve with extra raspberries and syrup.

Protein-Packed Waffles

Ingredients:

- 1 ½ cups oats, blended into flour
- 1 tbsp protein powder (optional)
- 1 tsp baking powder
- 1 tsp vanilla extract
- 1 cup milk
- 2 eggs
- 1 tbsp honey or maple syrup
- 2 tbsp peanut butter (optional)

Instructions:

1. Preheat your waffle iron.
2. Blend oats in a food processor to create oat flour.
3. In a bowl, mix oat flour, protein powder, and baking powder.
4. In another bowl, whisk together milk, eggs, vanilla extract, and honey.
5. Combine wet and dry ingredients until smooth.
6. Pour batter into the waffle iron and cook according to the manufacturer's instructions.
7. Serve with fresh fruit or nut butter.

Banana Nut Waffles

Ingredients:

- 1 ½ cups all-purpose flour
- 1 tbsp sugar
- 1 tsp baking powder
- 1 tsp cinnamon
- 1 ripe banana, mashed
- 1 cup milk
- 2 eggs
- ¼ cup chopped walnuts
- 2 tbsp melted butter

Instructions:

1. Preheat your waffle iron.
2. In a bowl, mix flour, sugar, baking powder, and cinnamon.
3. In another bowl, whisk together milk, eggs, mashed banana, and melted butter.
4. Stir the wet ingredients into the dry ingredients until smooth.
5. Gently fold in chopped walnuts.
6. Pour batter into the waffle iron and cook according to the manufacturer's instructions.
7. Serve with extra banana slices and syrup.

Spiced Pear Waffles

Ingredients:

- 1 ½ cups all-purpose flour
- 1 tbsp sugar
- 1 tsp baking powder
- 1 tsp cinnamon
- ¼ tsp nutmeg
- 1 ripe pear, peeled and diced
- 1 cup milk
- 2 eggs
- 2 tbsp melted butter

Instructions:

1. Preheat your waffle iron.
2. In a bowl, mix flour, sugar, baking powder, cinnamon, and nutmeg.
3. In another bowl, whisk together milk, eggs, and melted butter.
4. Stir the wet ingredients into the dry ingredients until smooth.
5. Gently fold in diced pear.
6. Pour batter into the waffle iron and cook according to the manufacturer's instructions.
7. Serve with a dusting of cinnamon sugar or whipped cream.

Lemon Ricotta Waffles

Ingredients:

- 1 ½ cups all-purpose flour
- 1 tbsp sugar
- 1 tsp baking powder
- 1 cup ricotta cheese
- Zest of 1 lemon
- 1 cup milk
- 2 eggs
- 2 tbsp melted butter

Instructions:

1. Preheat your waffle iron.
2. In a bowl, mix flour, sugar, and baking powder.
3. In another bowl, whisk together ricotta cheese, lemon zest, milk, eggs, and melted butter.
4. Stir the wet ingredients into the dry ingredients until smooth.
5. Pour batter into the waffle iron and cook according to the manufacturer's instructions.
6. Serve with fresh lemon slices or syrup.

Vanilla Bean Waffles

Ingredients:

- 1 ½ cups all-purpose flour
- 1 tbsp sugar
- 1 tsp baking powder
- 1 vanilla bean, scraped (or 1 tsp vanilla extract)
- 1 cup milk
- 2 eggs
- 2 tbsp melted butter

Instructions:

1. Preheat your waffle iron.
2. In a bowl, mix flour, sugar, and baking powder.
3. In another bowl, whisk together milk, eggs, melted butter, and the scraped vanilla bean.
4. Stir the wet ingredients into the dry ingredients until smooth.
5. Pour batter into the waffle iron and cook according to the manufacturer's instructions.
6. Serve with vanilla whipped cream or fresh fruit.

Blueberry Cheesecake Waffles

Ingredients:

- 1 ½ cups all-purpose flour
- 1 tbsp sugar
- 1 tsp baking powder
- ½ cup cream cheese, softened
- 1 cup milk
- 1 egg
- ½ cup blueberries
- 1 tsp vanilla extract

Instructions:

1. Preheat your waffle iron.
2. In a bowl, mix flour, sugar, and baking powder.
3. In another bowl, whisk together cream cheese, milk, egg, and vanilla extract.
4. Stir the wet ingredients into the dry ingredients until smooth.
5. Gently fold in blueberries.
6. Pour batter into the waffle iron and cook according to the manufacturer's instructions.
7. Serve with more blueberries and a drizzle of syrup.

www.ingramcontent.com/pod-product-compliance
Lightning Source LLC
LaVergne TN
LVHW081342060526
838201LV00055B/2812